BATS TO BLUEBONNETS

52 WEEKS OF HILL COUNTRY FUN FOR YOU AND YOUR CHILDREN

Special thanks to Sara Crutcher and Olivier who inspired the book and for the following who provided invaluable input: Frauke Bartels, Betty Crutcher, Martin and Vanessa de la Rosa, Oliver Franklin (branding exercise, page 57), Deidre Gantt, Alice Green, Julia Guzman, Julie Guzman, Anya Hanson, Bill Hanson, Troy Kimmel, KimCo Meteorological Services (weather activity, page 63), David Konstam, François Lévy, Claire Love, Peggy Love, Mary Love Parsley, Gabino Peña, Ali Turley (Capitol anecdotes), Tanya Voss, Cindy Wade and Mark and Mandy Winford.

Published by

ALLIE PRESS

2805 Robinson Avenue, Austin, Texas 78722 (512) 482-8537

Printed in the U.S.A.

Cover Design: Becky Veach
Book Design, Layout and Illustration: François Lévy

ISBN 0-9659921-0-1

CONTENTS

CHECK OUT THE EASY-TO-USE ACTIVITY AND DESTINATION INDEX IN BACK

ACTIVITY **PAGE**

CONTENTS

ACTIVITY **PAGE**

ACTIVITY **PAGE**

INTRODUCTION

Discovery. Oh, to be a child and live in a world of discovery. We, as adults, frequently get caught up in deadlines and obligations. We might see a spider web in the living room and think, "(sigh) I've got to get a broom and chair and take that down," only to have a child walk up behind us and say "Wow—a spider web!"

That children become adults with adult sensibilities is without question. The real question is, "How long do they retain a child's penchant for discovery?" How long before their thinking changes from, "There are a MILLION things I can do today!" to "I can't think of ANYTHING to do today; I guess I'll watch TV."

This book was inspired by the desire, the deep commitment, to facilitate discovery. More importantly, the intent is to facilitate the shared experience of discovery between children and their parents. This shared experience provides an opportunity to fall passionately in love with life and each other.

We have great empathy and compassion for parents who want a magical, passionate relationship with their children. We believe that parents are doing a great job and deserve a great deal of acknowledgement. With really busy schedules, we think that parents might welcome some ideas for fun that are memorable and don't necessarily take a great deal of time or cost very much. In fact, what we learned in researching this book is that we can come up with activities that occur in the midst of our existing routines so they don't have to take as much time.

Our selection of these Austin-specific ideas was dictated by several criteria: that the activity 1) be highly interactive to the extent it produces a "Wow!" exclamation, 2) provide the rare atmosphere for parents and children to fully express themselves and, 3) potentially awaken an interest or passion within a child such that she pursues it independently. Each set includes an activity that the parents and children can do together so as to share the discovery with their children, a suggested follow-up activity for the child to do himself and a list of resources. The activities are ordered sequentially by season with the year-round entries interspersed. See the seasonal index in the back of the book.

Enjoy! Parents, have as much, if not more fun than your children. Allow the sense of wonder in these activities to connect with the child that resides in all of us.

Additional information about most, if not all of the organizations featured in the book can be found on the net at **www.citysearch.com.**

Julie Wade
Ana-Alicia Konstam

We dedicate this book to our parents, Mr. and Mrs. Israel Peña and Mr. and Mrs. J.R. Wade, who helped to create the memories that made our childhoods special.

BATS GALORE

YOU & YOUR KIDS...

Sure, we know that Austin is home to the largest urban bat colony in North America, but have you taken your children to see the bats? **Between March and November,** 1.5 million Mexican free-tailed bats take up residence under the Congress Avenue bridge. It's a fascinating sight to behold to watch their nightly emergence. Bring a blanket, some snacks and make yourselves comfortable at the observation area behind the Austin-American Statesman. The deck of TGI Fridays within the Radisson is another prime viewing spot, not to mention the option of bat viewing aboard a Capital Cruise boat. Call the American-Statesman Hotline for viewing times.

ON THEIR OWN...

For the younger ones, here's a night-time activity. Suggest that they, like the bats, go out at night (to your backyard). Ask them to look around for insects, a bat's favorite food, using all of their senses. Have them tell you what they see, hear and smell that would be of interest to a bat.

BATS CONTINUED

For older kids, work with them to erect a bat house. Bat Conservation International (BCI) can provide information on purchasing a kit at their gift shop or by mail.

Note: It's best to wait two days after a heavy rain; **the baby bats begin to fly in August.**

Spring, Summer, Fall

FOR MORE INFO...

Austin American-Statesman
Bat Hotline: 416-5700 Ext. 3636
Bat Conservation International
(BCI) Phone: 327-9721
BCI Web site: www.batcon.org
Bat Watching on the **Capital Cruise:**
480-9264; Cost: Adults $8;
Seniors $6.50; Kids $5

GENERATIONAL JOURNALISM

YOU & YOUR KIDS...

Bring your children together with their grandparents, older relatives or long-time family friends. Encourage them to be journalists. Give them a tape recorder and have them ask questions. "What was it like when you were growing up? What did you do? Did you have pets? What did you do for fun? What was Uncle Bob like that reminds you of me? Why do you say I look like Mom?" The last two are good examples of questions that help kids recognize their place in the family. These tapes will become priceless and give your children precious memories of their elders.

ON THEIR OWN...

Suggest to your children that they create a book about their grandparents. Younger ones can use crayons and Big Chiefs. Older ones could use a computer. Encourage your child to keep a family scrapbook from his/her perspective. Give them the extra photos that you aren't going to use. Better yet, for family vacations or other special occasions, buy them a disposable camera, so they can take pictures of their own without your worrying about the camera. Their scrapbook will look very different from yours!

Year Round

STOP & SMELL THE ROSES

YOU & YOUR KIDS...

Here's an activity that doesn't take a lot of time, but soothes the soul in a big way. Drop by Zilker Botanical Gardens and smell your way through the rose garden. With over 100 varieties of roses, you can't leave the garden without being much more peaceful than when you arrived. Have your children pick the prettiest color, scent and any other ideas that they have. Ask them which rose is most like them and why. Rename that flower after your child. **Roses are in bloom from April through August; April and May feature the most outstanding display.**

ON THEIR OWN...

Start an annual ritual of having your child select one nicely scented plant to grow in your garden. Suggest that your child check out a book on aromatherapy and discover why this age-old art is being talked about once again.

Teach your children to dry bouquets of flowers. Simply bind the stems together with string or a rubber band. Hang upside down until they dry. Tie a ribbon around the stems and mount on a wall. Your family can enjoy these colorful, dried flowers for a long time to come. Note that the flowers should be hung to dry before they begin drooping or wilting.

Spring, Summer

FOR MORE INFO...

Zilker Botanical Garden: 477-8672
Location: 2220 Barton Springs Road
Hours: 7 a.m. - 7:30 p.m.
Cost : Free

URBAN ISLAND RETREAT

YOU & YOUR KIDS...

Find yourself stressed in the middle of town with a car full of irritable kids? Escape to a tranquil haven minutes from downtown Austin—Red Bud Isle on Town Lake. Drive as far as you can and walk to the tip of the island. Dip your toes in the cool water. You can hardly hear an automobile. Listen for the call of the birds, the distant roar of the dam. Imagine that you're in the middle of the countryside. Heaven for half an hour.

Let's treat it like the gem that it is. Bring a large trash sack and collect some trash. Lead your kids in a scavenger hunt: for example, "collect 2 paper cups, 3 aluminum cans, 4 pieces of paper," etc. with the one coming closest winning a special treat. Before you leave, make sure and skip some stones across the water.

Encourage your children to look for flat, smooth rocks suitable for painting (use acrylic paints) once they return home. Pebbles are the right size for a nose, ears or eyes. These paper weights never go out of style as far as grandparents are concerned.

Year Round

FOR MORE INFO...

Red Bud Isle: To Get There: Take MoPac to Lake Austin Boulevard and head west. Take a left at Red Bud Trail, the light after Exposition and just before the LCRA. You'll immediately encounter the bridge over Town Lake and the teeny, tiny Red Bud Isle on your left.

GO FLY A KITE

YOU & YOUR KIDS...

Attend the annual Kite Flying Contest at Zilker Park. Held the first Sunday of March at the soccer fields, this is very much a family event. All manner of contests are featured, including largest and smallest kites. The most unusual, steadiest and most creative categories are divided into two divisions—16 and over and 15 and under. Perhaps your children would like to participate in one of these competitions.

One of the most memorable aspects of the day is not the kites entered in the sanctioned contests but the hundreds flown by the crowds just for the fun of it. So, bring along a kite to fly with your children.

Also, the Northwest Recreation Center has a terrific Kite-Making Workshop a few weeks before the contest. Make five different kites to bring home.

ON THEIR OWN...

Encourage your child to make a kite by forming a diamond (as in baseball field) of any size with a cross piece. Cover with paper, attach a tail and string. Voilá! It can be as simple as starting out with drinking straws to form the diamond.

For older children, here is a more ambitious kite:

Figure 2

Oriental Paper Bag Kite

1. Cut out a circle from stiff cardboard.
2. Cut out the center of the circle to make a ring.
3. Tie three short pieces of string to the ring.
4. Then tie the strings together (figure 1).
5. Trace the inside of the ring on the bottom of a paper bag.
6. Cut out the hole.
7. Glue the ring inside the bag, with the strings coming out of the hole (figure 2).
8. Decorate the grocery bag and attach a long kite string. Now you can run with it or tie it to a tree and watch it fly.

Figure 1

FOR MORE INFO...

Austin Parks and Rec: 499-6700
Northwest Rec Center: 458-4107
Kite Workshop Cost: $1 adults; $.50 children

DISCOVER THE TREES

YOU & YOUR KIDS...

You now have one more reason to hike through Austin's great system of trails and parks. The Forestry Department recently completed a program named *Trails of Trees.* Eight parks feature trails with trees marked and identified. A *Trails of Trees* book will be available in late 1997 and will likely be posted on a website. Call for info.

In your own neighborhood, combine a leisurely walk with a discovery tour of trees right in your midst. Use the *Trails of Trees* book or a pictorial tree reference as your guide. Half Price Books is always an inexpensive source for reference books. See how many trees you and your children can identify. Make a game out of it: "How many different trees do you think we can find today?"

ON THEIR OWN...

When grandparents and other doting adults are around, make a point of encouraging your child to provide a tour for these friendly grown-ups, pointing out as many trees as he or she is able. Of course, adults must ooh and aah at this display of knowledge.

Encourage your child to collect leaves, perhaps pressing and drying them in a book and then mounting (gluing) them in a notebook. Book markers can also be made by mounting the dried leaves on heavy paper and covering the front and back with clear adhesive paper, commonly known as "contact paper."

Perhaps your family would like to volunteer for the various TreeFolks' plantings which take place during **October through March.** Call for information about other volunteer opportunities as well. You can always plant a tree in your own yard.

Spring, Summer, Fall

FOR MORE INFO...

City of Austin Forestry Department: 476-6485
TreeFolks-ReLeaf: 443-5323
Trails of Trees **Parks:** Shipe Park, Pease District Park, Catherine Lamkin Arboretum at Rosewood Park, Becker Elementary School, Stacey Park, Zilker Park, Town Lake Trail, Mayfield Park. For park locations, call **Austin Parks & Recreation** at 499-6700 and request the Parks and Recreation Official Map/Brochure and Facilities Guide.
Half Price Books: 3110 Guadalupe, 451-4463; 2929 S Lamar, 443-3138; 8868 Research, 454-3664

STROLL WITH THE PEACOCKS

YOU & YOUR KIDS...

Share with your children utter tranquility in the middle of Austin. Stroll through the gardens of Mayfield Park and admire the exquisite beauty of the peacocks. Do your children know how to tell the males and females apart? Hint: the male is the colorful one!

Deeded to the City of Austin in the 1970s, the Mayfield-Gutsch home and surrounding gardens are maintained primarily by "The Friends of Mayfield Park." Extraordinary flower beds have been "adopted" by volunteers who spend many weekends planting and maintaining their individual beds of native species. There are several hiking trails surrounding the gardens. This is a lovely setting for a picnic.

ON THEIR OWN...

Make sure that you have at least one native plant in your yard or have your child plant one. Challenge your child to see how many native plants he or she can name as you are driving around town.

Encourage your child to start a piggy bank and make contributions or donate time to The Friends of Mayfield Park. Volunteering sets a very strong example for young, formative minds.

Year Round

FOR MORE INFO...

Mayfield Park, 3505 West 35th Street, west of MoPac just before Laguna Gloria Museum
Hours: Daily, 10:00 am - Dusk
Austin Parks and Recreation: 499-6700
Friends of Mayfield Park:
Call Barbara at 477-6031
To Donate money towards the restoration of the house and gardens: Mail checks to **The Mayfield Park Project,** 2704 Macken, Austin, TX 78703

FRESH FROM THE FARM

YOU & YOUR KIDS...

Go to a farmers' market and buy some fresh vegetables. Try Whole Foods on Wednesday afternoons from 2:30 - 6:00 p.m. There is also a farmers' market in south and east Austin, as well as the Travis County Farmers Market which is open daily. Sit down with your children and some cookbooks and encourage your child to plan a menu using the fresh vegetables. Cook this special meal together.

ON THEIR OWN...

Have your child plan one meal per week that you cook together. Mealtime can be stressful for busy families. Share the responsibilities with your children and take the opportunity to cultivate an appreciation for cooking. You might have a budding chef on your hands.

Spring, Summer, Fall

FOR MORE INFO...

Farmers' Markets in the Austin Area:
Whole Foods Market, 6th and Lamar: Wednesdays, 2:30 - 6:00 pm; **Travis County Farmers' Market,** 6701 Burnet Road: 8:00 - 6:00 pm daily **East Austin:** call Sustainable Food Center at 385-0080 for info; **South Austin:** 3000 S. Congress (in a parking lot—look for the sign), Saturdays, 8am - 1pm

FIRE WORKS

YOU & YOUR KIDS...

Give your children a glimpse into the exciting world of fire fighting. Set up a tour of a fire station. There is flexibility in the time and location of the tour. Simply call ahead to make arrangements. Back at home, enact a fire drill; have your children select a place outside your house to meet, such as the mail box.

ON THEIR OWN...

We all forget to test smoke detectors. Delegate this responsibility to your children. Three publications are available from the Austin Fire Department: *Fire Extinguishers, Smoke Detectors,* and *Fire Safety and Survival.* Your children can learn a great deal from these sources and make recommendations around your home to insure safety.

Year Round

Austin Fire Department: 448-8302

CREATE A GARDEN

YOU & YOUR KIDS...

Drive around Austin looking for interesting landscapes. Have your children identify their favorite styles of landscaping, plants and flowers and photograph them. For the very youngest, have them identify the colors in the rainbow as you drive around. Spring is a wonderful time to catch different varieties in bloom, though fall is a good time for planting also.

For additional inspiration, take the Spring Garden Tour featuring twelve of the most unique private gardens in Austin. Sponsored by Austin Community Gardens, the event is always held the weekend of Mothers' Day.

ON THEIR OWN...

Give your older child his own bed in the yard to design, plant and maintain. Remember, a bed can be as small as an area surrounding the base of a tree with a cluster of a single type of flower. The photographs and a trip to the library for landscape design books will provide the ideas. For younger children, give them the opportunity to select a single plant by going to the nursery and offering them a few choices from which to pick. You can plant it together.

Also consider, in an effort to keep the cost down, swapping cuttings with a neighbor or friend outside the neighborhood. If you don't feel comfortable working with cuttings, all the better. Have your child locate a neighbor who's a gardener. Gardeners LOVE to share what they have and, even more so, enjoy teaching youngsters to garden. Ask your neighborhood association to promote a block cutting swap. It's a great opportunity to meet neighbors.

Spring, Summer, Fall

FOR MORE INFO...

Zilker Botanical Garden: 477-8672 Location: 2200 Barton Springs Rd; Hours: 7 p.m. - 7:30 p.m. Cost: Free. Inquire about the many weekend activities to support the gardening enthusiast, as well as the annual spring event, Florarama.

Austin Community Garden: 458-2009 Spring Garden Tour Cost: $5/person, Mothers' Day Weekend

MOVIES UNDER THE STARS

YOU & YOUR KIDS...

There are two really fun ways for you and your children to see movies during the summer. The City of Austin Parks and Recreation features movies at area swimming pools beginning in late May through mid August. What could be more fun for kids than watching movies while they swim? For a list of participating pools and the scheduled Saturday evening dates, call Austin Parks and Recreation.

Another regional favorite is watching movies at the Rocky River Ranch in Wimberley. Weekend evening showings are featured from Memorial Day to Labor Day. From the comfort of your lawn chairs and for the reasonable price of $2.50 per person, you and your children can enjoy the closest experience to our childhood memories of a drive-in movie. A thirty-year tradition, movies begin at "dusk thirty." Call Rocky River for movie listings and dates.

ON THEIR OWN...

How about a movie written, directed and produced by your children? For younger children, involve them by asking that they make up a story to be made into a movie or even have them tell a story or sing a song which you videotape. This could be a 1-2 minute movie. If your child is ready for a more advanced activity, they can write a script and operate the camcorder themselves. Regardless of how elaborate the movie, a "show time," concession stand and tickets are a must. Don't forget the credits. Write the actors' names and crew information on cards to be held up and filmed at the end.

Summer

FOR MORE INFO...

Austin Parks and Recreation: 476-4521

Rocky River Ranch: (512) 847-2513

To Get There: From MoPac, connect with 290W. At the Y in Oak Hill (290 and 71 intersection) take 290W for about 13 miles. At Drip;ping Springs, look for Hwy 12 at a traffic light. Turn left and travel 15 miles, driving through Wimberley. On the edge of town, turn left onto Hwy 3237 and go .5 mile. Take a right onto Flight Acres Road. The Corral Theater is on your right.

FAMILY TIES

YOU & YOUR KIDS...

Discover along with your children your family's past. The Texas State Library's genealogy section recommends several things. Draw up a family tree. Have one of your children take notes and write down Dad's name, birthdate, birthplace, marriage date and place of marriage. Then, write down grandfather's name, birthdate, birthplace and marriage date and do the same with grandmother. Now on Mom's side, go through this exercise again.

ON THEIR OWN...

Have each member of the family tree provide a piece of material from one of their articles of clothing. Your child could either sew the pieces together to make a pillow, or braid them together to make a belt or headband. For older kids, use the information from the tree to create a work of art. Use symbols or icons that are associated with the individual. For example, if grandfather likes to fish, draw a colorful fish.

Year Round

FOR MORE INFO...

Texas State Library, Genealogy Department: 463-5463
Library Location: 1201 Brazos
Hours: Tuesday - Saturday, 8:00 - 5:00
For additional family history research:
Toad Hall Bookstore will order *My Family Tree Workbook* for $2.95; call 323-2665
Church of Jesus Christ of Latter-Day Saints Family History Center: 837-3626
Location: 1000 Rutherford Lane
Hours: Vary on weekdays; Saturday hours 9:00 - 3:00

HILL COUNTRY PRESIDENT

YOU & YOUR KIDS...

Not many cities can boast of a presidential library or the rare treasure of a former first lady the likes of Lady Bird Johnson. Spend a few hours at the LBJ library. Your car enthusiasts will enjoy the 1968 "stretch" presidential limousine and a recreation of the family's 1910 Model T Ford. Perhaps you would like to pick up some presidential paper dolls at the gift shop for your younger ones to enjoy. Make sure your children know that LBJ was born just a few hours away and that, when he was a boy, no one expected him to be president. Ask your child what he thinks it would be like to grow up and be president.

For a more extended outing, take a drive out to the LBJ boyhood home in Johnson City or the Ranch east of Fredericksburg. Ranch tours are available daily, departing from the LBJ State Park in Stonewall. Known as the Texas White House during LBJ's term in office, the ranch tour sometimes includes chance encounters with the Johnson family.

ON THEIR OWN...

Suggest to your child that he or she write a letter to the President of the United States at

1600 Pennsylvania Ave., Washington DC 20500. For folks online, the email address is: president@whitehouse.gov. There is a White House website especially for kids:

http://www.whitehouse.gov/wh/kids/html/home.html

Year Round

FOR MORE INFO...

LBJ Library: 916-5137;
Hours: 9 a.m. - 5 p.m. daily except Christmas;
Location: 2313 Red River
Parking: Free
LBJ Ranch: 210/868-7128
Ranch Tours: $3 per person; 6 and under free
For State Park Info: (210) 868-7128

OUTDOOR MUSIC

YOU & YOUR KIDS...

Attend an outdoor concert and bring along a frisbee, your dog and a picnic dinner. There is a smorgasbord of venues. Call for times and featured musicians. When you look around and see the diverse mix of music fans, you will experience the heart and soul of the Austin music scene; all are equal when appreciating music.

ON THEIR OWN...

Give your children an opportunity to play some instruments. Austin Symphony Children's Day Art Park takes place every Wednesday morning in June and July from 9:30 - 12 noon at Symphony Square. The kiddos can experiment with all kinds of musical instruments. So much fun, and it's free!! There is a nominal 50 cent charge for adults. Perhaps working mothers can take a half day off and participate with their children in one Wednesday activity. Be sure and arrive a little early, because it's first come, first served. Encourage your children to make their own music.

Spring, Summer

FOR MORE INFO. . .

Outdoor Music Venues

Wednesdays, May-June—Auditorium Shores: **Austin Parks and Recreation:** 499-6700

Every other Wednesday, June-August—**Blues on the Green** at the **Arboretum:** 338-4437

Thursdays, April-October—**Shady Grove Restaurant:** 474-9991

Sundays, May-June—Zilker Hillside: Austin Parks and Recreation: 499-6700

Weekends, Year Around—**Central Market Cafe:** 206-1000

Children's Day Art Park Info—Austin Symphony Orchestra: 476-6064

Location: 1101 Red River

Children must be accompanied by an adult. Cost: Children free; Adults 50¢

HILL COUNTRY PEACHES

YOU & YOUR KIDS...

Do you remember when you were a child, and there was something your family ate seasonally every year? Maybe it was watermelon out on the back porch or homemade ice cream with everyone taking turns sitting on the ice cream freezer as someone else turned the crank. Here in the Hill Country, you can create some family memories of your own by serving up peaches in your own special way. If you want to, you can make an annual event out of buying the fruit in Fredericksburg or Stonewall. Pack up the kids and spend a summer afternoon in the country during the harvest season between June and July. Drop by a peach stand where they don't just sell peaches. There's peach ice cream, peach cobbler, peach... Well, you get the idea. If you want to stay a little closer to home, you can pick your own peaches at Schwegmann's Orchard located in Georgetown.

Another Hill Country favorite is Luling watermelon. Attend the three-day Watermelon Thump Festival in June. Call for details.

ON THEIR OWN...

Have your son or daughter locate a recipe and make a peach dessert (with or without your help, depending on their age). The Austin American-Statesman always features recipes around peach harvest time in June or July. Plant a peach tree in the backyard. Fall is the time for planting.

FOR MORE INFO...

Fredericksburg Visitor Information: (210) 997-6523
To get there: take 290 West through Dripping Springs and past Johnson City. Keep heading west, and you'll encounter Stonewall, then Fredericksburg.

Schwegmann's Orchard: (512) 863-3314
To get there: take IH-35 north; on the north side of Georgetown, take exit 264 and continue north on the east side service road for 1.5 miles.

Watermelon Thump Festival: 210/875-3214; first night free!

Summer

CHILDHOOD GAMES

YOU & YOUR KIDS...

Unless you speak with your children about your childhood, they won't know how you spent your time. Teach your children the games that you played, whether it be marbles, jacks or hop scotch. Check out a book from the library if you need help recalling.* Think back and remember what it felt like when you were able to get all the way to tensies in jacks, or you were the winner at four square. Relive these fond memories with your children. They are dying to know what you were like as a child. Encourage your children to write a booklet of these activities, so they will be passed on to their children.

ON THEIR OWN...

Hopscotch is a game that shouldn't be lost to our children. Here are the instructions:

- Using chalk, draw the diagram as illustrated.
- Each player must have a marker—a rock, bottle cap, etc.
- To start, player one stands outside the court and tries to throw his/her marker on space 1. If the marker touches any lines, the player loses a turn.
- After the marker lands correctly, the player hops onto the court, hopping on 1 foot for a single box and using both feet for two boxes side by side.

- The player hops to the end, turns around and hops back, picking up his/her marker.
- The other players follow, making sure not to step on a line or hop in a box with a marker, which results in forfeiture of your turn. Next time around, this player would repeat the marked space.
- After all players have had their first turn, the first player now throws the marker into space 2 and hops through the diagram accordingly.
- The first player to navigate all the spaces successfully wins the game.
- Once the players have been through the court once, another round is begun. Every time a player gets through the court successfully, he or she initials the space in which the marker rests. Other players may no longer step in that space, but the player to whom it belongs may stand in it on both feet.

Some other games to consider include making mud pies in a pie tin; Red Rover, and the hand game "Oh Mary Mac, Mac Mac."

Year Round

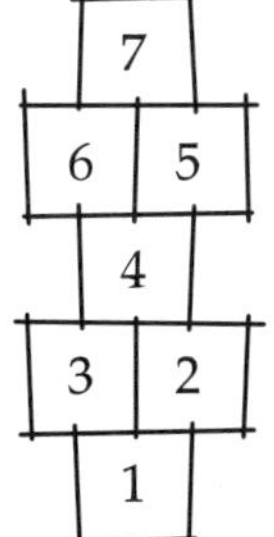

Hopscotch, Hangman, Hot Potato and Ha Ha Ha: A Rulebook of Children's Games* by Jack Maguire is available from the **Austin Public Library.

OLÉ

YOU & YOUR KIDS...

Austin has long been a city that openly celebrates multiculturalism. Take advantage of the many opportunities to experience the Hispanic culture. There are three important days of celebration. Cinco de Mayo (May fifth) is associated with independence from France. Dies y Siez de Septiembre (September 16) marks independence from Spain. Also look for interesting goings on for the Dia de los Muertos (Day of the Dead) on November 1. All dates are celebrated with numerous activities at Fiesta Gardens Park and other venues in Austin. The Capitol is often the scene of a mariachi band on one of these dates. For specific activities, which vary from year to year, check the Chronicle, Austin-American Statesman's *XLent* on Thursday or Statesman's *Best Bets* the day of the holiday. Mexic-Arte and Galeria Sin Fronteras are two galleries featuring Hispanic art and cultural exhibits. Mexic-Arte specifically offers children's events and workshops such as mask making or puppetry. Call for info.

ON THEIR OWN...

Check out a Spanish-language tape series from your library and suggest that your son or daughter learn 10 phrases that can be used over dinner. Then plan a Mexican or Latin American meal and encourage the entire family to make basic requests in Spanish. Suggested phrases: Enjoy your meal—Buen provecho; pass the salt and pepper please—pasa la sal y la pimienta por favor; the food is very good—¡La comida está muy buena! or ¡La comida está deliciosa!

Spring, Fall

FOR MORE INFO...

Fiesta Gardens Information: 499-6700 or 499-6720. Location: 2101 Bergman; from IH-35, take Holly Street (the first exit north of the river) east; take a right on Chicon, and you will run into Fiesta Gardens.
Mexic-Arte Museum: 480-9373. Location: corner 5th Street and Congress. Hours: 10 am-6 pm M-F.
Galeria Sin Fronteras: 478-9448. Location: 1701 Guadalupe Street. Hours 11 am-6 pm T-Sa.

THE SHAPE OF THINGS

YOU & YOUR KIDS... Take a tranquil walk through the Umlauf Sculpture Garden & Museum where over 130 works by the internationally known artist and former University of Texas professor are on display. For "kid fun," request a treasure map. After your wee ones locate and circle the sculptures on their map, they can exchange it for a prize. Think back to your childhood experience of sculpting something with your hands; perhaps it was in scouting or an elementary school art class. As you and your child walk through the garden, wonder aloud what it would be like to be able to sculpt like Mr. Umlauf and what your child would sculpt if he could make anything he wanted.

ON THEIR OWN... Suggest a sculpting activity. Provide your children with a bar of soap and a ball-point pen. Ask them to decide what they would like to "sculpt" and have them draw it on the soap. Coloring books are a good reference for younger children, and a fish is one of the easiest subjects to start with. Next, carve along the lines and, Voilá— a sculpture! For the youngest children, use Play-Doh™.

Year Round

Umlauf Sculpture Garden: 445-5582. Hours: Th, Sa, Su 1-4:30 pm; Fr 10 am-4:30 pm. Cost: Adults $2.00, Students $1.00, Under 6 free. Directions: from Lamar and Barton Springs Road, head west on Barton Springs, turn north to 605 Robert E Lee.

GO FOR THE STARS

YOU & YOUR KIDS...

Escape the city lights for a look at the sky lights and foster the sense of wonder we've always had for the twinklers. Check out one of numerous opportunities to star gaze. Monthly "moonlighting" tours take place at Wild Basin. Advance reservations are encouraged for this highly popular event. The Austin Astronomical Society is a great source for additional activities throughout the year. Finally, the Painter Hall Observatory at UT Austin is open to the general public for guided telescope viewing every Saturday evening; times vary during the year.

Do your own star gazing tour at Mount Bonnell. Parents can point out constellations to younger children; as children get older, they can point out constellations to the parents.

ON THEIR OWN...

Have your child draw the multiple phases of the moon. Start with the new moon. Four days later, draw the small crescent seen in the western sky. Go out every day about the same time (7:00 pm) and draw the moon as it increases in size and moves eastward. When it once again becomes a full moon, it will be located due east.

More appropriately for younger children, have your kids demonstrate an eclipse using a flashlight behind a plate. This is especially fun when you see an eclipse outside and then create your own eclipse indoors.

Year Round

FOR MORE INFO...

Wild Basin Wilderness Preserve: 327-7622
Location: 805 N Hwy 360, 1 mile north of Bee Caves Rd
Moonlighting Tour Cost: adults $3.00; K-12 $1.50; pre-kindergarten free.
Austin Astronomical Society: 252-2966
Austin Astronomical Society web site: http://www.main.org/aas
Painter Hall Observatory: 471-5007
Painter Hall Location: 24th Street between Speedway and Inner Campus Drive.

A BUTTERFLY GARDEN

YOU & YOUR KIDS...

Walk through the Butterfly Trail at Zilker Botanical Garden. Explain to your children that if you grow certain flowers or plants, butterflies will come to your yard, because you have created a "home" or habitat for them. This is a great opportunity to talk about how our yards are not just ornamental; many different insects and birds need a place to live, just as we do. Look through your children's eyes and see what you discover in your backyard.

ON THEIR OWN...

Have your older children check out a book on butterfly gardening and plan a garden. Encourage them to identify the visiting butterflies. Perhaps you could have your younger children choose one plant from the following list which you could then help them plant. Have them draw the butterflies they see. Note that butterflies are most prevalent in the hottest months. Once you have some flowering plants, you will be amazed how quickly the butterflies come.

Use the following list of butterfly friendly native plants as a guide*.

Agarita
Buttonbush
Coreopsis
Mexican Oregano
Spirea
White Mistflower

Butterfly Bush
Canna Lily
Flowering Sedum
Passion Flower
Texas Star Hibiscus
Yarrow

Butterfly Weed
Carolina Jessamine
Lantana
Pavonia
Verbena

Summer (best), Spring, Fall

FOR MORE INFO...

Zilker Botanical Garden: 477-8672 Location: 2220 Barton Springs Road. Hours: 7:00am - 7:30pm. Cost: free.

* The **City of Austin Environmental and Conservation Services Dept.** (499-2199) publishes a free Water Conservation Packet which includes the handout *Xeriscape for Wildlife.* **Texas Parks & Wildlife Nongame and Urban Program** publishes *Butterflies and How to Attract Them to Your Garden*, as part of the comprehensive Backyard Habitat Packet No. 1. Call 389-4974 to request. Cost: $15.

HEALTHY GROUND

YOU & YOUR KIDS...

Research composting and build a compost pile. Some key points to remember are:

- Attempt to use equal amounts of "greens and browns."
- Mix together a variety of ingredients; you can include food, but no meat.
- Shred or chop all ingredients if possible for faster decomposition.
- Build the pile large enough to retain heat.
- Turn or aerate the heap regularly to let in air.
- Water regularly to keep the pile as moist as a damp sponge.

Austin Community Gardens offers workshops every other month. Call for dates and times. Feel free to call and ask any composting or gardening questions. You can find out everything you need to get started.

ON THEIR OWN...

Appoint your children the "Keeper of the Compost." Have your children make the daily "contributions" to the compost pile. THIS IS IMPORTANT: help them pick out some gloves and/or a hat that they always wear when they carry food out to the compost pile. In so doing, the trip to the compost pile will seem to be an important ritual, and children LOVE rituals and playing roles. When it's time for spring planting, be sure to show your children how the composting has produced terrific soil. Have them help you add the soil to beds and prepare for planting.

Year Round

Austin Community Gardens: 458-2009.

DISC GOLF

YOU & YOUR KIDS...

Hitch up your sleeves, grab your frisbee, and take your kids for a round of disc golf. Note: you gotta call it Disc Golf and never Frisbee Golf! Played similar to golf, each course consists of a series of holes laid out so that when the player completes one hole, he proceeds to the beginning of the next hole until the entire course has been played. Conventional golf is measured by the number of strokes per hole. In disc golf you count the number of disc throws it takes to complete the hole (basket). Your score is the cumulative number of throws, and the low score wins. First-time players, don't keep score; just have fun and discover muscles that you haven't used in years! For younger kids, bypass the course and go straight from pole hole to pole hole. You may want to start them off by throwing the frisbee to your dog.

Courses in Austin (no charge):

Zilker Park:	2100 Barton Springs Road
Pease Park:	1100 Kingsbury St. (south and west of Lamar Boulevard at 24th Street)
Bartholomew Park:	5201 Berkman Drive
Mary Moore Searight Metropolitan Park:	907 Slaughter Lane

ON THEIR OWN... If you have some Disc Golf Professional wannabees, help them design a course in your backyard or neighborhood. Your back yard may only have room for one or two holes; however, look around in your neighborhood and you might find space for a four or five hole course.

Year Round

FOR MORE INFO... Discs can be purchased at local sporting good stores. For a more personal introduction to the sport, David Douglas Moody is a very helpful and knowledgeable player who has a shop at the Pease Park course. Look for him in the parking lot south and west of Lamar at 24th street. Mr. Moody will be happy to guide you as you select your first golf disc.

THE GOVERNOR IS IN

YOU & YOUR KIDS...

Tour the Governor's Mansion and learn which governor didn't live in the mansion after it was built. Find out which two governors were married—to each other!

Visit the historic State Capitol with its new addition. Call ahead and make arrangements to meet with your state representative. Since it is always open, a late-night visit to the rotunda is fun for all ages. Some people say there are ghosts. Actually, the rumor got started when an Austin newspaper reported in 1915 that workers heard "wailing" sounds; it was reported the next day the sounds were made by a dog trapped inside the Capitol trying to get out! What do your kids think about ghost in the Capitol? Have them listen carefully and deliver their verdict. Take a drink from one of the eight spigots of the circa 1928 granite water fountain on the eastside grounds. Now connected to the municipal water supply, up until 1980 the fountain bubbled up mineral water long believed to possess medicinal powers.

ON THEIR OWN... What would your kids do if they were the governor of Texas? Encourage your son or daughter to write a letter to the governor to let the governor know how he/she is doing!

FOR MORE INFO...

Year Round

Governor's Mansion: 463-5518
Tour Times: M-F am, every 20 minutes beginning at 10:00 with the final tour starting at 11:40.
State Capital Tours: 463-0063. Tours occur daily except Christmas, Thanksgiving and New Year's Day; every 15 minutes from8:30 am- 4:15 pm weekdays and 9:30 am- 4:15 pm weekends. Meet just south of the rotunda.
Cost: no charge for either tour
Note: bring quarters for the parking meters
Governor's Address: P.O. Box 12428, Austin, TX 78711

EYE ON ARCHITECTURE

YOU & YOUR KIDS...

Promote an appreciation within your children for architecture. Spend some time on the weekend (when parking isn't as challenging!) at the University of Texas and take a leisurely walk around the campus; be sure and visit the interiors of these architectural treasures. How do different rooms make your children feel? How do you suppose the buildings' designers achieved these effects? Are the spaces comfortable, awe-inspiring, dramatic, or dynamic? How do elements like views, control of light and materials, and decoration reinforce those feelings? Bring along your camera and take some photographs of the buildings.There are many, many outstanding examples to see. All the better if there is a building under construction.

ON THEIR OWN...

Expose your children to the work of architecture students. Walk through the Mike and Maxine Mebane Gallery inside Goldsmith Hall (just south of the Union) which displays student works and traveling exhibits.

Encourage your children to draw the façade of a building using a photograph. Architects use mathematical proportioning systems to lend beauty and grace to their designs; see if your children can find the geometries of the building's façade by identifying simple geometric shapes—such as squares and arcs of circles.

As you go about town, have your children look for these geometric shapes in buildings they see. For those expressing further interest, invite them to design a building of their own on paper or in 3D. Some "building materials" to use are popsicle sticks, Legos, cardboard or even a deck of playing cards. How many floors can they build?

Year Round

FOR MORE INFO...

Campus maps are available throughout the campus including the Tower and Visitor Center. **UT Visitor Center:** 471-6498. Visitor Center Hours: M-F 8 am-4:30 pm. *Brick by Golden Brick,* by Margaret Berry, is an historical look at UT architecture and is available on a reference basis at UT's Perry Castañeda Library or the School of Architecture Library in Goldsmith Hall.

THE WORLD OF STAINED GLASS

YOU & YOUR KIDS...

Drive around Austin and stand in awe before some outstanding displays of stained glass. Some suggestions include a number of churches: St. Mary's Cathedral, St. Julia's Catholic Church, Gethsemane Lutheran Church, and Our Lady of Guadalupe Catholic Church. Keep an eye on stained glass as you make your way about town and find your own favorites. Explain to your children how stained glass is created—an artist develops a design; colored glass is scored and broken; the glass is then soldered together using strips of lead.

ON THEIR OWN...

Encourage your children to try their hand at stained glass. There are a variety of "faux" stained glass activities. For the young ones, use plastic wrap (Saran wrap), permanent markers, and 2 paper pie plates. Cut a piece of plastic wrap no larger than the paper plate; have your children color in sections of the plastic wrap using the markers until the entire area is colored; cut a hole in the 2 paper plates and glue the plastic wrap between the plates to frame the "stained glass."

Kits can be purchased at Michael's in which the children paint onto a hard plastic form to mimic the stained glass look.

Year Round

FOR MORE INFO...

St. Mary's Cathedral: 476-6182; corner of 10th and Brazos (metered parking).
St. Julia's Church: 926-4186; 3010 Lyons Street.
Gethsemane Church: 836-8560; 200 West Anderson Lane
Our Lady of Guadalupe Church: 478-7955; 1206 E. 9th Street
Michael's: 795-8573, 10225 Research; 448-2633, 801 Wm Cannon; 331-5656, 13945 N. Hwy 183, 328-6142; 3201 Bee Caves Road.

LOOK FOR THE STORY

YOU & YOUR KIDS...

Check out some of the many murals in Austin. A diverse sampling of murals include the following: an elephant and zebra mural at 816 Lamar (a kid favorite); Fiesta Gardens pool house; Hickory Street Bar & Grill; Tower Records; and Renaissance Market. You can make a day of it, or simply include one of these as a minor detour as you go about your evening or weekend. Of course, there are many others; the entire family can be on the lookout, and you will discover favorites of your own. As you study the art, explain to your children that murals tell someone's story. Ask them to imagine what the story is behind the mural. If you feel this is too advanced, play "I Spy," locating various objects and asking your children to find them in the mural.

ON THEIR OWN...

Encourage your children to express themselves via a mural. Murals begin on paper, so ask them to tell a story by drawing it on paper. Older children will be ready to paint on a surface, such as a tree house or the inside of your garage. Long lengths of butcher paper can also be used and then mounted on bedroom walls.

Year Round

FOR MORE INFO...

The elephant & zebra mural: 816 12th Street, 2 1/2 blocks east of Lamar.
Fiesta Gardens: 2101 Bergman; from IH-35, take Holly Street (the first exit north of the river) east; take a right on Chicon, and you will run into Bergman; head right for the pool house.
Hickory Street Bar & Grill: NW corner, Congress & 8th Street.
Tower Records: NW corner of 24th Street & Guadalupe.
Renaissance Market: 2300 block of Guadalupe, just south of Bevo's Bookstore.

IN your NEIGHBORHOOD

YOU & YOUR KIDS...

If you grew up in a small town or even lived for a long period in the same neighborhood in a city, you remember the feeling of community—people knowing each other's names and playing with the kids in the neighborhood. Teach your kids to be involved in your immediate community and attend a neighborhood association meeting. Some neighborhoods host some really fun events. There are several July 4th parades featuring kids, adults, dogs, etc. on skates, bikes and in wagons. Attend one of these and, better yet, start one in your own neighborhood. Call the City of Austin to determine a contact for your neighborhood association.

ON THEIR OWN...

Volunteer along with your children, or as they get older, encourage them to volunteer on their own. Bake cookies with your children for the neighborhood association meeting. Most associations have a newsletter which needs to be folded and delivered. Ask the newsletter editor about including a "kids' corner" which could feature articles written by children. Perhaps your neighborhood picks up trash or could be encouraged to do so.

Finally, there is always an elder person who needs help with the yard, a perfect opportunity to adopt another "grandparent." In the process of volunteering, you and your children will meet some terrific people who live around you.

Summer, Year Round

FOR MORE INFO...

City of Austin Neighborhood Association Information:
499-2584 or 499-2692

Travis Heights July 4th Parade:
Starts at 10 am at St. Edward's Univ., just north of the Main Building and proceeds down Eastside Drive ending up at Stacey Park.

WATER AWARENESS

YOU & YOUR KIDS...

Did you know that Texas is expected to experience water shortages in some part of the state by the year 2020? Some years produce drought-quantities of rainfall, and other seasons yield monsoon rains. During a particularly wet year, we might think our water troubles are gone, but it is really only a matter of time. This is why one of the greatest gifts you can give to your children is an appreciation for water and water conservation practices. Order a water conservation packet from the City of Austin if you are an Austin resident. If you live outside of Austin, contact your MUD to inquire.

Here's a couple of water-awareness activities to engage your child interactively. Numerous agencies utilize volunteers to monitor water quality. The City of Austin has a"Water Watchdog" program focusing on creeks. What a great way to educate children about water quality issues and, more importantly, connect them with their environment! Other water-quality monitoring programs include the Texas Natural Resource Conservation Commission and Travis County Creek Watch. The training, time commitment and flexibility vary greatly. If this is something that interests you as a parent, you will need to call around and look for the program that is right for you. If you do volunteer and you take your children with you as "assistants," they will truly be inspired by you.

TNRCC provides a publication entitled *Watershed Owner's Streamwalk Guide* which is used in their volunteer program; you could use some information to take your children exploring in a creekbed. An additional publication entitled *Do You Know How to Keep Our Water Clean?* is specifically geared towards children and is a terrific way to introduce these topics.

Another awareness-building activity to share with your children is to design your own way of sustaining Austin creeks—even if it is simply picking up trash. Make sure your children know these are OUR creeks to take care of. Ask them, "I wonder what we could do to keep the creeks healthy?"

ON THEIR OWN... Encourage your children to come up with a target list of water-saving actions your family can take.

WATER CONTINUED

Look for ways that water is conserved, as well as how water is wasted as you drive. For example, if you see someone watering midday, you can explain that water evaporates during the sunlight hours and not as much after sundown. Together, learn to identify native plants and look for them as you drive.

Year Round

FOR MORE INFO...

City of Austin Environmental & Conservation Svcs. Department (to order a water conservation packet): 499-2550

Water Watchdog Information—City of Austin: 499-2088

TNRCC Texas Watch: 239-4782

Travis County Creek Watch: 708-4460.

TNRCC (to request *Watershed1 Owner's Streamwalk Guide,* Pub. #GI-218 or *Do You Know How to Keep Our Water Clean?,* Pub. #GI-27): 239-0028.

SPENDING A DAY WITH DAD

YOU & YOUR KIDS...

Make sure that your children occasionally spend a day with their dad, uncle, grandfather or male family friend. The Dallas Cowboys' Training Camp in July and August is a favorite sports activity. For a night straight out of a bedtime story, the Elisabet Ney Museum's Fairy Tale Ball the last Saturday in June encourages children to dress up in fairy tale costumes and features a costume parade, a professional ballet performance and storytelling that will make this a night to remember.

ON THEIR OWN... Moms, encourage your children to write their dads a letter at least once a year, possibly on Father's Day, but probably appreciated even more so for no special occasion at all!

Year Round, Summer

FOR MORE INFO...

Dallas Cowboys' Training Camp: 416-5858
Elisabet Ney Museum: 458-2255
Fairy Tale Ball: last Saturday in June
Cost: free.

THE GOOD OLE DAYS

YOU & YOUR KIDS...

Take your kids back in time to the Hill Country in the late 1800s. Drive out to Pioneer Farm and give your children an opportunity to milk a cow, feed animals and cook over a fire or wood-burning stove. Make some butter, grind some corn or hold a baby chicken in your hands. Besides being open every Sunday afternoon, annual special events take place in September (Fall Festival), Halloween and the Christmas season which feature additional activities. Note the additional summer hours. Consider volunteering as a family.

ON THEIR OWN...

After your visit to the farm, suggest that your children do something commonly done by pioneers—encourage them to make a branding iron of their own. Here are some examples of Texas brands. Point out that people often used combinations of letters or symbols. Ask them to design a brand on paper, thinking about what symbols or letters are unique to them. Then, to make the branding iron, draw the design on cardboard and carefully cut it out. Then get a long dowel (round piece of wood) and glue it on the end. Or take a large potato, cut it in half, and carefully carve your design. Remember to carve the potato in reverse, since you will be printing the brand from the potato. Dip the potato or the cardboard brand in paint, and print it on paper using tempera or acrylic paints. Discover the many things which can be branded!

Year Round

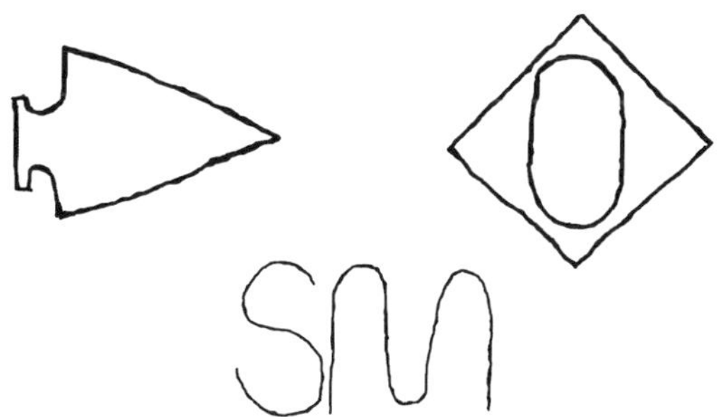

Some well-known Texas brands.

FOR MORE INFO...

Jourdan-Bachman Pioneer Farm:
837-1215

To Get There: N on IH-35; take the Braker exit (2 exits north of 183) and head east; take a left at the 'T' intersection onto Dessau Road; go about .5 mile and turn right at the Pioneer Farm sign on Sprinkle Cut-Off Road; the farm is .5 mile down the road on the right.

Hours: Year round—1pm-5pm Sundays; June-August: 9:30 am-3 pm M, T, W, Th; September-May: 9:30 am-1 pm M, T & W.

Cost: \$3-adults; \$2-3-12 years; \$2-groups of 10 or more.

CELEBRATE AFRICAN-

YOU & YOUR KIDS...

Experience the rich heritage of African-American culture. Folktales, a bookstore specializing in African-American literature, presents storytime every first Saturday of the month from 11am-noon. During Black History Month in **February,** there are a myriad of opportunities around town, particularly Huston-Tillotson College and George Washington Carver Museum. Call for info. Mitchie's Fine Black Art is a cultural treasure, offering special events, speakers and programs during February, Juneteenth and throughout the year. The Rosewood Recreation Center is the site of **June** 18 and 19 Juneteenth events. The Intergenerational Festival on June 18 features games, carnival rides and gospel music. June 19 includes a parade, poetry readings, music and dance. Check the *Austin Chronicle, Austin-American Statesman's* XLent and the *Statesman's* Best Bets (back of Section B) for information during February and for Juneteenth.

ON THEIR OWN...

Recommend that your child read about the African-American celebration Kwanzaa, the home-centered gathering which honors both Africa and

America. The seven day **December** observance reinforces the history of African American culture and emphasizes history as a source of empowerment. Many children's books are available at your branch library. Your child will discover that, like Hanukkah, Kwanzaa is a very rich, celebration of family and culture, incorporating symbols which acknowledge the dignity of a unique race of people.

Again, like Hanukkah, this is best experienced in the home of friends. With your children, look for an opportunity to share this holiday with another family.

Winter, Summer, Year Round

FOR MORE INFO...

Folktales Bookstore: 472-5657
Location: 1806 Nueces
Rosewood Rec. Center: 472-6838
Huston-Tillotson College: 505-3000
George Washington Carver Museum: 472-4809
Mitchie's Fine Black Art: 323-6901
Location: 5312 Airport Blvd.

NATIVE AMERICANS

YOU & YOUR KIDS...

Attend the annual Pow Wow held in **November** at Tony Berger Stadium. Native American dancing, arts, and other cultural presentations are featured throughout the day.

Take your children to the Native American exhibit at the Texas Memorial Museum. North American Indian culture is displayed dating back to 15,000 BC. Your children will no doubt be surprised by the deck of cards made from rawhide. Ask your children to look for what we share in common with the Native American culture. Perhaps you and your children have used a kayak similar to the one on display.

ON THEIR OWN...

Here is an activity which honors the Native American culture. Older children will be able to handle this on their own; the youngsters will need some help. Dreamcatchers, which look like spider webs, are Native American devices designed to "net" bad dreams and let the good dreams wriggle through—a great way to address "bad" dreams.

How the Dreamcatcher Came to Be

The Ojibway Indian parents believed the night air was filled with good and bad dreams waiting to come to the sleeper. Parents would hang a dreamcatcher where the baby(ies) slept. Bad dreams, not knowing the way, would get hopelessly lost and tangled in the webbing. There they would perish and burn off like dew in the first light of dawn. Good dreams would find their way through the hole in the middle of the dreamcatcher to the sleeper.

Dreamcatchers are about 4-5 inches in diameter, have a pheasant feather hanging from the bottom, and usually feature a fetish (charm) strung in the webbing, such as a bear, turtle, bird, etc.

Supplies:
2 pipe cleaners
yarn—5 feet of crocheting yarn, ribbon or packing string
beads
feathers

1) Fold in the ends of the pipe cleaners, so younger children won't scratch themselves.
2) Twist the pipe cleaners together end-to-end to form a circle.

3) Set aside one foot of the yarn.
4) Knot one end of the remaining yarn to the circle. Loop the yarn through the circle and over the opposite side. Continue looping in a random pattern, creating an open web effect.
5) When you run out of yarn, tie a knot.
6) Use extra yarn to tie beads, feathers and other decorations onto the web.
7) Hang wherever dreaming takes place.

Fall, Year Round

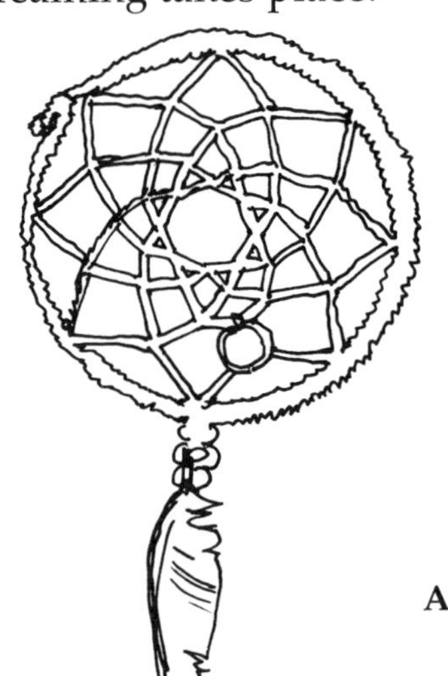

FOR MORE INFO...

Texas Memorial Museum
Hours: M-F, 9 am- 5 pm; Sa, 10 am- 5 pm; Su, 1 pm- 5 pm.
No admission fee; contributions welcomed.
Location: UT Campus
Call 471-1604 for parking info and directions.

AISD American Indian Education Project: 414-3849
Pow Wow Price: free.

FISCAL FITNESS

YOU & YOUR KIDS...

Contact your bank about a tour of the vault. Your child will be fascinated by the massive door and countless stacks of money. It's hard to remember, but we adults were awed by banks the first time we entered one.

To foster the ability to manage money, help your child set up an account in his or her name. Encourage them to make deposits no matter how small. Perhaps they can save towards Christmas presents or college. For younger children, a piggie bank is more appropriate. Draw up an official-looking balance sheet to be decorated by your son or daughter. Give them a deposit slip and make an entry for each deposit. If they are too young to count, draw pictures of the coins, and have them color the coins to be "deposited."

ON THEIR OWN...

If your child is interested in earning money, encourage him or her to be creative. Here are some ideas: a lemonade stand, recycling cans, mowing yards, feeding the neighbor's animals, and clipping coupons and being "rebated" for the amount saved. There are children who draw and sell artwork in their neighborhood. Let them surprise you.

Year Round

WEATHER WATCH

YOU & YOUR KIDS...

Spend some time in the fascinating Weather Gallery at the Austin Children's Museum. You and your children can observe a "touchable" tornado and a demonstration of wind velocity.

ON THEIR OWN...

Encourage your child to pull back the curtains at home and watch a lightning show. Buy a rain gauge for tracking the rainfall and suggest that they listen to the weather report to see how different parts of town receive vastly different amounts of rain. Allow your children to play in the rain (when there is no lightning)!

For the older elementary-aged child, Troy Kimmel recommends making a barometer to help them (and probably you!) understand the concept of air pressure. Necessary supplies include: a wide-mouthed jar, a balloon, rubber band and coffee stir stick or small straw. Cut and remove the tapered end of the balloon so that the balloon will then fit over the lip of the jar; place the rubber band around the lip of the jar on top of the balloon; place some glue on the mid section of the balloon and affix the stir stick horizontally so that it extends from the mid part of the balloon top to off the side several inches; it may be necessary to tape the stir stick to the balloon while the glue dries. Once it has dried, you now have a barometer. Air is trapped *inside* and will reflect the pressure *outside*. As pressure lowers outside, the stir stick will point downward indicating low pressure. As pressure rises on the outside, the balloon is pulled inward, and the stir stick points up indicating rising pressure. Air pressure is the weight of the mass of air above us at any given point on the earth's surface. Air pressure is significant to weather forecasters, because high pressure is usually characterized by fair skies while low pressure can be associated with stormy, cloudy weather.

Year Round

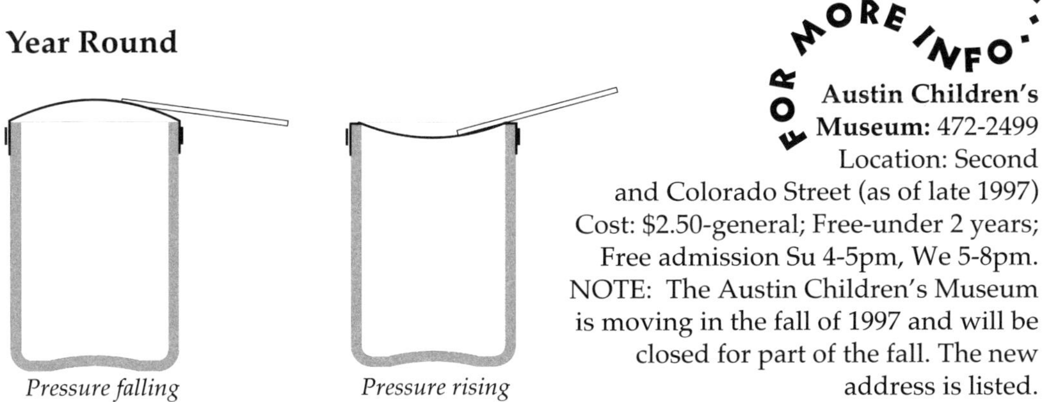

Pressure falling *Pressure rising*

Austin Children's Museum: 472-2499
Location: Second and Colorado Street (as of late 1997)
Cost: $2.50-general; Free-under 2 years; Free admission Su 4-5pm, We 5-8pm.
NOTE: The Austin Children's Museum is moving in the fall of 1997 and will be closed for part of the fall. The new address is listed.

A STEP BACK IN TIME

YOU & YOUR KIDS...

Experience with your children what it was like to live in the time of their great grandmother. Visit the Republic of Texas Museum and walk through the hands-on exhibit depicting frontier life where, together, you will discover why people bathed outside, how food was kept cool without a refrigerator, and how your great grandmother washed clothes. Ask for a tour, and, if the museum staff is not too busy, you will be given an outstanding one. "Hands on" includes walking through a covered wagon, donning clothing and hats worn by our forefathers, and climbing atop a saddle. The kids will love it!

ON THEIR OWN... Have your children think about their grand children and great-grand children. Ask them to put together a notebook of stories and pictures, explaining what life was life back in the 1990's. Remind your children that they have to explain in detail, because in the future, how we live today will be just as foreign to our future offspring as the life of our pioneer forefathers is foreign to us.

Year Round

FOR MORE INFO... **Republic of Texas Museum:** 339-1997; 510 E. Anderson Lane. To Get There: from IH-35, take exit 240A; head west on Anderson (Highway 183); the museum is the building just west of the Four Points Motel which is located at the northwest corner of IH-35 & 183.
Hours: M-F, 10am-4pm; S, 11am-4pm
Cost:$2 adults; $.50 children

HEROES AMONG US

YOU & YOUR KIDS...

Heroes come in all shapes and sizes, and sometimes they can seem difficult to find. Introduce your children to some historical figures who are larger than life at the Republic of Texas Museum. Find out what James Fannin said just before he was defeated at Goliad and William B. Travis' infamous words as he drew a line in the sand with his sword at the Alamo.

Continuing with the theme of heroism, the museum features an exhibit of courageous individuals who persevered against all odds—genuine heroes who were common, ordinary people being extraordinary when they were called to be.

ON THEIR OWN...

Make sure your children know someone doesn't have to be a comic book super hero or a Walt Disney movie star to be a hero. Ask them to look around and look for extraordinary people. Who are their heroes? And if your children were heroes in their own lives, what sorts of things would they be doing? If you introduce this conversation, you will give them something to think about for years into the future. They might ask you in return, "Who are your heroes?"

Year Round

FOR MORE INFO...

Republic of Texas Museum: 339-1997; 510 E. Anderson Lane. To Get There: from IH-35, take exit 240A; head west on Anderson (Highway 183); the museum is the building just west of the Four Points Motel which is located at the northwest corner of IH-35 & 183.
Hours: M-F, 10am-4pm; S, 11am-4pm
Cost: $2 adults; $.50 children

EMBRACE ALL CULTURES

YOU & YOUR KIDS...

Experience cultures from at least five continents at the annual Race Unity Day. Held the second Sunday in June, the free event features various stage performances, as well as a children's area with arts and crafts representative of different cultures. International food and beverages are also available.

Additional multicultural opportunities include numerous festivals in Austin. St. Elias Church sponsors a Mediterranean Festival the second weekend in October; taste Ethiopian, Greek, Italian and Arabic food. The French Legation hosts a Bastille Day celebration during the weekend closest to July 14, the actual date of the historic holiday; experience French food, music and dancing. Pflugerville's main square is the site of the German Deutschen Pfest the third weekend in May. Austin Children's Museum sponsors International Children's Festival, a full day of around-the-world cultural fun in September.

ON THEIR OWN...

Have your children select a country and go to the library and check out some books on food, culture and dress. Your children can select the food to be prepared with your appropriate guidance depending on their age. Encourage the whole family to dress according to the customs and learn and use a few phrases during the meal. This will be a big hit with your children. Put them in charge.

If your child is interested in writing to someone in another country, have them contact the World Pen Pal Association.

Spring, Summer, Fall

FOR MORE INFO...

Mediterranean Festival / **St. Elias Eastern Orthodox Church:** 476-2314

Bastille Day / **French Legation:** 472-8180

Deutschen Pfest / **Pflugerville Parks and Recreation:** 251-5082

Race Unity Day / **Baha'i Faith:** 448-5444.

International Children's Festival / **Austin Children's Museum:** 472-2499.

World Pen Pal Assoc.: P.O. Box 337, Saugerties, NY 12477 (914) 246-7828.

RIDE A DILLO

YOU & YOUR KIDS...

Children who don't often ride public transportation love riding the bus. The next time you are downtown, suggest to your children that you take a ride in a Dillo. The round trip from Palmer Auditorium to the Capitol will take about 45 minutes, and you and your children will see things that you've never noticed before. Your kids will enjoy riding al fresco and standing in the back. Here's an opportunity to enjoy the beautiful view of Congress Avenue. Why not do this during the holidays between Thanksgiving and New Year's Day when the avenue is festively decorated? You never know, Santa might be on board!

Use a Dillo for hard-to-find-parking events such as July 4th, Aqua Fest, or Pecan Street Festival. Capital Metro can give you route information.

ON THEIR OWN... Ask your child why a growing city like Austin benefits from having mass transit. You might be surprised at what they have to say.

Year Round

FOR MORE INFO...

Capital Metro Route Schedules:
474-1200

Note about parking and bus route: During the week, park in the free parking provided east of Palmer Auditorium and south of City Coliseum. To travel up Congress Avenue, take the #86 Congress/East Capitol route which runs every 10 minutes from 6:30 am until 7 pm. From 7-9 pm, the trolley runs every 20 minutes.

ECO EXISTENCE

YOU & YOUR KIDS...

Drop by the Austin Nature and Science Center and use an eco-detective kit to heighten the discovery when you walk the trail along the pond. Stops along the trail feature an audio station which, when activated, plays different sounds of critters in this area, frogs for example. The kit includes a pair of binoculars with which to look for the corresponding animal. There's a great deal to discover at the center. You'll want to return with your children again and again.

In your own backyard, you can give your children an opportunity to observe an ecosystem. Stake out a small area with a string perimeter, perhaps 3 feet X 3 feet (the younger the child, the smaller the area). Have them observe for 15 minutes. If they are older, have them either sketch or list in a notebook everything they see, including plants, animals, rocks, water, light and anything else they notice. For example: "There is a grasshopper, a ladybug, a black bug about 1/4 inch long with pincers on his head." Ask them to include what the insects are eating and anything else they notice. For younger children, simply have them tell you what they see or have them play nature bingo. Draw nine boxes on a card and draw items like butterfly, flower and lady bug; three across or up and down wins.

Now, explain to them that in an ecosystem there is a food chain where everything has an interdependent purpose. Ask them to imagine what other kind of bug or plant might exist in this ecosystem. What would it look like? What would it eat? Encourage them to draw a picture.

ON THEIR OWN...

Ongoing observation could include the following activities for your son or daughter to do by his or herself:

- Ask them daily or weekly what has changed.
- Create a poster of the marked-off area, continuously adding to the drawing.
- Encourage them to check out a book from the library which would allow them to identify species by name and define the place in the food chain.

FOR MORE INFO...

Austin Nature & Science Center:
327-8181
Location: 301 Nature Center Drive (from Lamar, turn west onto Barton Springs; turn right onto Stratford Drive, between the soccer fields and Zilker Botanical Garden; follow the road as it curves around; park under the overpass; the Nature Center is across the street. Suggested donation is $2 adults & $1 children

Spring, Summer, Fall

NATURE'S BALANCE

YOU & YOUR KIDS...

"Nobody makes a greater mistake than he who did nothing because he could only do a little."

—Edmund Burke
British Statesman and Orator
Quoted in the "Diversity Endangered" Exhibit
The Texas Memorial Museum

Austin is well known for the passions surrounding environmental issues. Spend an hour or two at The Texas Memorial Museum on the University of Texas campus. Expose your children to the native animals in Texas, including "The Alcove," a child-pleasing exhibit that reveals night-prowling species in their nocturnal habitats.

Also on the third floor check out the "Diversity Endangered" exhibit which not only explains the issue of diversity but, more importantly, gives your children some actions that they can take to make a difference in this arena.

ON THEIR OWN...

Have your children take one action recommended in the "Diversity Endangered" exhibit.

Request the free Macintosh software entitled "Vanishing Species" and have your child share at the dinner table about an endangered species . (PC software will be available at some point in the future.) Alternately, encourage your child to check out a book from the library about an endangered specie featured in the exhibit. The good news is that some animals previously on the list are no longer considered endangered.

FOR MORE INFO...

Year Round

Texas Memorial Museum
Hours: M-F 9 am- 5 pm;
Sa, 10 am-5pm; Su 1 am-5pm.
No admission fee but contributions welcomed.
Location: UT Campus
Call 471-1604 for parking info and directions.

TALL TALES

YOU & YOUR KIDS...

Raconteur: One who recounts stories and anecdotes with skill and wit.
—American Heritage Dictionary

Living in Texas we have the responsibility of sustaining the legendary storytelling abilities of our forefathers! Educate your children early and take them to hear a professional storyteller. All of the major bookstores in town, as well as branch libraries feature free story times on a regular basis.

The best place to hear stories is around a camp fire, and Travis County Parks Department sponsors "fireside tales" at various parks. Call for information.

ON THEIR OWN...

Now, find out just how imaginative the storytellers in your family are. Encourage your children to create a story together. The first person starts off with a single sentence. The next person adds an additional sentence. And on it goes. The more outrageous the better. See how long they can keep it up. Perhaps your children will begin to create stories without your prompting!

Don't forget to read a nightly bedtime story to your children.

Year Round

FOR MORE INFO...

Book People Bookstore: 472-5050
Barnes & Noble Booksellers: 418-8985 (Arboretum area), 328-3155 (Westlake Hills)
John Henry Faulk Central Library (to determine branch library in your area): 499-7599
Travis County Parks Department: 473-9437
Cost of Travis County "Fireside Tales": $5 per vehicle.

AN AUSTIN WALKABOUT

YOU & YOUR KIDS...

Enjoy some fine architecture and be entertained by stories of Austin's past on one of several walking tours. You may not think this would be interesting for everyone, but exercise both you and your children's imagination. Ask them what they think Austin looked like back then. Imagine the horses and buggies in the streets, women strolling down the sidewalks in their hoop skirts.

Take advantage of the Congress Avenue and Sixth Street Tour and discover the history of the Avenue and the entertainment district. The Bremond Block Tour features a remarkable group of Victorian homes in a single block dating from the 1850s - 70s. Located between 7th and 8th streets and San Antonio and Guadalupe streets, the homes originally belonged to members of a single family. Both tours are 1 1/2 hours.

ON THEIR OWN...

Encourage your son or daughter to design a tour (walking tour or car tour) of his or her favorite activities. When grandparents, relatives or friends visit from out of town, you have a ready made tour guide.

Better yet, have your young guide provide a tour for YOU and see Austin through a child's eyes. If you do this, remember, kids are used to the adults calling the shots. To jump start their comfort with designing the entertainment, ask them to start with one destination—their favorite place. Ask them to do so on a regular basis, and you won't have to worry about their saying, "I don't know what to do". The only trick is you gotta go anywhere they say and make them feel you love it!

FOR MORE INFO...

Free Walking Tour Booklets available from Visitors Center.

Austin Visitors Center: 478-0098

Location: 201 E. 2nd Street

Congress Avenue & Sixth Street—Departs promptly from the south steps of the State Capitol at 9 a.m. Thursday - Saturday and 2 pm on Sunday March 1 - November 30.

Bremond Block Tour—Departs from the south steps of the Capitol at 11 am on Saturday and Sunday; March 1 - November 30.

Spring, Summer, Fall

A RESTING PLACE

YOU & YOUR KIDS...

Dispel the childhood myth that cemeteries are scary and explore our rich heritage. There are many local cemeteries to choose from, several featuring some very old grave sites. Rubbings are a favorite with children of a wide range in ages. Simply bring along some paper and crayons. Pose the question to your children, "I wonder what it was like to live during the time of this person."

The newly restored State Cemetery at East 7th and Comal streets features guided tours, or you can use a brochure to route your own tour. Drop by the cemetery office to pick up a map of famous grave sites which is also available at the Austin Visitor Information Center. Use the brochures to help you locate the resting place of Stephen F. Austin, Ma Ferguson and John Connally or pick your own favorite historical figures.

Some other cemeteries to visit between the hours of 9 am - 5 pm, M-S:

Oakwood	1601 Navasota
Memorial Park	2800 Hancock
Evergreen	3304 E 12th
Plummers	Springdale & E 12th

ON THEIR OWN... Encourage your children to find other surfaces on which to do rubbings—coins, trees, window screens. See what other surfaces they come up with and make sure they save their rubbings in a scrapbook.

Year Round

FOR MORE INFO...

State Cemetery: 463-0605
State Cemetery Office: 909 Navasota
Call ahead for guided tours.
Austin Visitor Center: 478-0098
Visitor Center Location: 201 East 2nd Street.

WATCH IT GROW

YOU & YOUR KIDS... Pack up your children and go visit a farm. Boggy Creek Farm, located just a few miles east of IH-35, features just-picked, organically grown produce throughout the year except for December through March. The farm stand is open to the public Wednesdays from 9 am-1 pm and Saturdays from 9 am-2 pm. Depending on the season, herbs, strawberries, broccoli, lettuce and sweet corn are but a few of the produce selections.

ON THEIR OWN... Encourage your child to ask questions about organic gardening while at Boggy Creek Farm. Help them to do any other research about organic gardening. Depending on their age, suggest that they either plant a single plant in a pot or, for older children, "give" them a small 3 foot by 3 foot plot where they can tend some vegetables. Some easier vegetables to grow include black-eyed peas, green beans and peppers. If you have extra produce, share with a neighbor or a homeless organization.

Spring, Summer, Fall

FOR MORE INFO... **Boggy Creek Farm:** 926-4650. Location: 3414 Lyons Road To get there: From IH-35, go east on 7th Street; take a left on Pleasant Valley; go four blocks and turn right onto Lyons. Homeless Organizations: **HOBO:** 476-4357. Other Farms: **Crown Nest Farm:** 926-3311, 9501 Springdale.

LIGHTS FANTASTIC

YOU & YOUR KIDS...

Celebrate the coming of Christmas with an annual Austin favorite—the 34th Street light show. With virtually every house participating, the block between Guadalupe and one block to the east, Home Lane, the street is truly magical. Expect a major traffic jam, so parking and experiencing the lights on foot is recommended. Make the evening more festive by bringing along hot cocoa and playing Christmas carols. Come on. It's Christmas!

Other annual favorites include the Zilker tree lighting around the first of December with free music and festivities. The Zilker Trail of Lights is a display of where your child can sit on Santa's lap. Avoid the traffic by taking a shuttle from Barton Creek Mall.

ON THEIR OWN...

Have your children design a Christmas light display. For younger children, it may be choosing the color of a string of lights for one small bush. Older children will be able to take on a more elaborate display.

FOR MORE INFO...

Zilker Park: 472-4914
Location: 2100 Barton Springs Rd.

Winter

MARCH TO THE MUSIC

YOU & YOUR KIDS...

Nothing says fall in Texas like high school football! You may have forgotten the excitement, so this is an opportunity to relive it. One of the best festivities of game day is a marching band. Here in Austin, not only do we have high school but college ball. A band practice features enough pageantry to thrill almost any younger child, and most older ones will enjoy the rarity of being among so few spectators. Most high school bands are worth a visit; call the high school band office. UT's Longhorn Band practices throughout football season. Call the Longhorn Band for more information.

ON THEIR OWN...

Let your children make music. For the younger ones, try the following. **Cymbals:** two pot lids. **Chimes:** tie nails to a stick (using different size nails and different lengths of string) and strike them with a spoon. **Drum:** decorate an oatmeal box or a coffee can with a plastic lid. Use a spoon for a drumstick. **Hummer Kazoo:** fold a piece of wax paper over a comb. Press the wax paper and comb against your lips and hum a song. **Flute:** use the point of a pencil to poke holes in one side of a paper towel tube. Cover one end of the tube with wax paper. Hold the wax paper in place with a rubber band. Hum into the uncovered end of the tube as you move your fingers over the holes. **Tambourine:** decorate two paper plates or pie tins. Put some seeds or beans on one plate. Staple, tape or punch holes and string the plates together. Add some paper or ribbon streamers.

For older children, search garage sales and thrift shops to buy the real thing.

Record your children playing music. Have them design their cassette artwork, so their picture and/or name is featured just like professional musicians.

FOR MORE INFO...

Longhorn Band Office: 471-4093
Practice Days and Times: Mondays, Tuesdays, and Thursdays, from 6:30-8:30 pm; the location varies from year to year.

Fall

CHASING WATERFALLS

YOU & YOUR KIDS...

Combine a scenic drive with the pure delight of a natural swimming hole and experience Hamilton Pool. After an invigorating 1/4 mile hike, you will encounter a breathtaking limestone grotto with a 60-foot waterfall.

Share this historic information with your children. It all started 150,000 years ago with a 3-layer formation—sycamore sand collected to form the bottom level; the middle layer was hammett shell, and the top level was "cow creek limestone." The two bottom layers eroded due to the high water level within the limestone top layer which caused the bottom two layers to collapse. The limestone's ability to retain water sustains the waterfall.

ON THEIR OWN...

If you want to demonstrate to your children how limestone weathers naturally, this exercise requires two household items: an antacid tablet such as Rolaids and some vinegar. The antacid tablet is calcium carbonate, which is the chemical that makes up the mineral calcite in limestone. If you pour a weak acid (in this case, vinegar) over the tablet, it will fizz and become soft as it slowly dissolves. This is what happens when limestone is exposed over many years to the natural acids in rainwater.

FOR MORE INFO...

Hamilton Pool:
264-2740
Hours: 9 am-6pm; no admission after 5:30
Cost: $5 per vehicle
Location: Connecting either from 290W or FM 2244, take Highway 71 west and continue 1 mile past RR 620. Turn left on Hamilton Pool Road (watch for the sign) and drive 13 miles to the entrance.
You need to know:
For everyone's safety, **NO DIVING.**
No drinking water available.
No pets, glass containers, cooking, fires, fishing or overnight camping.
Swimming except after heavy rains; call to confirm.
Nature tours are available though you must call ahead to arrange.

Year Round; Summer for swimming

PITCH A TENT

YOU & YOUR KIDS...

Camp as a family at one of Travis County's many fine parks. You may be thinking you're not the camping kind. Try and remember when you were a child and the outdoors was fascinating. There were sounds you couldn't identify, and, well, even lizards were fascinating. Camp at the same place annually and start a tradition, or find a new adventure each year.

Since kids so enjoy being in the outdoors, perhaps you could more frequently have a simple cookout at one of the city parks. Your children will tell you; food tastes better when it's cooked outside, away from home. Hot dogs or hamburgers anyone? As they get older, your kids can write up the list of food to take, you can check it, and they can then pack it up. Try to do this in the evening, so you and your children can tell scary stories.

ON THEIR OWN...

Have your older children camp in the backyard all by themselves. For the younger ones, build a tent indoors with a sheet placed over several chairs.

Have your children "cook" and serve an outdoor meal for you. For older kids, sandwiches are doable. For the younger ones, Cheez Whiz and crackers can be a most impressive dinner.

Year Round

FOR MORE INFO...

Travis County Parks: 473-9437
City of Austin Parks and Recreation: 499-6700
Request the Austin Parks and Recreation Official Map/Brochure and Facilities Guide.
To request your copy of Texas Public Campgrounds Guide, call the **Texas Department of Transportation** at 1-800-452-9292 and press 2.

LIFE IS A STAGE

YOU & YOUR KIDS...

Enjoy the many talented Austin actors in one of the numerous, and usually free, outdoor productions. Zilker Hillside Theater presents a musical in July-August. Additionally, Shakespeare in the Park productions are offered throughout the year. Pack your blanket and dinner and kick back and relax. Try to sit up close if you have young children.

As you attend performances like these, talk to your child about how the characters on the stage are make believe, though they can teach us things about our own life. Listen for what the performance makes you think about, share with your child and ask what he thinks about this.

ON THEIR OWN...

Encourage your child to pursue a performance art by regularly performing for you. We all tend to think performance art is limited to the few and the talented. Help dispel this myth by facilitating weekly living room productions. Perhaps starting with the ABCs song will lead to other things like puppetry, dancing, singing or things you and I wouldn't think of. You should perform also so they know it's safe. When your children are at the age where they learn "Twinkle, Twinkle," this is the time to build their confidence for expressing themselves in front of people. You will vastly increase the likelihood that they will retain the confidence to pursue a public art form or speak publicly in front of people as they move into adulthood.

Spring, Summer, Fall

FOR MORE INFO...

Zilker Hillside Theater Information:
479-9491 or 499-6700
Shakespeare in the Park Information:
454-2273 or 499-6700. Location: 2100 Barton Springs Road

BABY TALK

YOU & YOUR KIDS...

Newborn babies are simply magnificent. Take a short break from your errands, visit the hospital nursery and witness the joy of new birth. Before you go, call the hospital closest to you to make sure they have some newborns in the nursery. Most infants stay in their mothers' rooms. You'll want to make sure that there are at least a few babies who are being bathed and monitored prior to rejoining their mothers. Just about any age child will be awe struck, not to mention the adults! Plus this is a good opportunity to talk to your child about his birth. Note that Columbia St. David's and Seton Medical Center appear to consistently deliver the largest number of babies. Also note that children are typically introduced to hospitals in painful situations. This is an opportunity to expose them to a hospital in a positive way.

Keep your ears open for new parents within your neighborhood, church or circle of friends. Offer to bring by some food, run errands. Depending on your children's ages, perhaps they could mow the yard, draw a card or some other thoughtful gesture. New parents will appreciate this more than you can imagine, since they may not have family in town.

ON THEIR OWN... Perhaps your family would like to make and contribute some baby blankets to any one of numerous organizations providing support to high-risk newborns: Caritas, CEDEN, Center for Battered Women or Volunteer Services at Brackenridge Hospital.

If you don't have a baby in the house, perhaps you have a youngster who would appreciate setting up a baby's room or area using a doll, baby's bed, diapers, etc. Your young nurse or doctor can check in on the "baby." Encourage your older daughter OR son to think about baby sitting.The American Red Cross offers baby sitting classes which prepare sitters to react in an emergency as well as play with different age groups. The 9-hour course costs $22.

FOR MORE INFO...

Columbia St. David's Medical Center: 476-7111
919 E. 32nd Street
Seton Medical Center: 323-1000
1201 West 38th Street
Brackenridge Volunteer Services: 480-1675
Caritas of Austin Social Services: 472-4135
CEDEN Family Resource Center: 477-1130
Center for Battered Women: 385-5181
American Red Cross: 928-4271

Year Round

FOR THE BIRDS

YOU & YOUR KIDS...

Discover the exotic world of The Sanctuary, an aviary featuring over 120 exotic birds. The 1.5 acre compound is easily navigable via a trail with bird cages on either side. Mature landscaping makes for a pleasant walk with surprises lurking around the corner. Though primarily featuring birds, several species of exotic animals including wallabies, pinto reindeer, and llamas are at home as well. Bring a picnic, but do so during the cooler times of year.

Open your child's eyes to the bird sanctuary right in your own backyard. Did you happen to see an unusual bird outside your kitchen window? Call your child and snatch a few precious minutes by sharing the spectacle. Encourage your son or daughter by picking up a bird handbook at the library or Half Price Books with which to identify as many species as possible. This could become enough of a passion that your child would engage in this practice when you're not around. Really!

ON THEIR OWN...

Entice the feathered creatures by hanging a very simple feeder constructed with a pine cone or rice cake, some string, peanut butter and bird seed. Tie the string to the pine cone or rice cake; apply peanut butter; "dip" the cone or rice cake in the seed which will stick to the peanut butter; tie your bird feeder to a branch and wait for the birds to come. Encourage your children to draw pictures of the birds in a book and imitate their calls.

Spring, Summer, Fall

FOR MORE INFO...

The Sanctuary: 288-2199
Open year around;
Tu-Su noon-6 pm
Cost: adults $4, children $2; seniors $3.
Directions: Take 290 west, continuing for another 2.2 miles past the 'Y' at Oak Hill. Watch for the signs at the 3rd traffic light south of the 'Y' and take the tricky left turn up the incline.

Travis Audobon Society Alert: 926-8751(for upcoming field trips, rare bird sightings, etc.)

Half Price Books: 3110 Guadalupe, 451-4463; 2929 South Lamar, 443-3138; 8868 Research, 454-3664

A FLOWERING FRENZY

YOU & YOUR KIDS...

Each spring the first wildflowers burst forth, bringing a timeless reminder of nature's seasonal generosity. Find your own rituals to celebrate. Take wildflower drives with your children and teach them how to press and dry the flowers. Call the Texas Department of Transportation's wildflower hot line and find out where the most outstanding displays of color are for the particular day of your outing. Take along a large book and some newspaper. Simply take a piece of the newspaper and fold it in half; place the flower inside and press it as flat as you can; place inside the book. Once you're back home, stack 4 or 5 heavy books on top of your "wildflower press" book. The flowers should be dry in 1-2 weeks, depending on humidity. The National Wildflower Research Center presents The Little House, a Saturday afternoon program of activities focusing on native plants guaranteeing lots of fun. Come any time during the three-hour period; parents must accompany children.

ON THEIR OWN...

Encourage your child to press other treasures of nature found in your own backyard, for example, leaves. Perhaps he/she would like to identify species of wildflowers or leaves. Check out a book from the library. Who knows? Maybe you have a future botanist or landscape architect on your hands!! Have the younger ones mount the dried flowers on construction paper and produce a work of art or make a greeting card for a special relative or friend. Or they can make bookmarks using "contact" paper (clear adhesive cupboard liner).

Note: when you pick flowers, please pick sparingly from a large cluster of blooms as opposed to picking the flower which stands alone. This will help ensure repropagation for next year.

Spring (best time); Summer

National Wildflower Research Center:
292-4200
TXDOT Wildflower Hotline: 832-7125
The Little House: Saturday, 1-4pm.
Cost: $3.50 adults, $2 for 5 and up, $1 under 5.

SEASONAL INDEX

Year Round

Spring

Summer

Fall

Winter

GROUP FUN

- Mitchie's Fine Black Art Gallery Tours—323-6901 (excellent)
- Amy's Ice Cream Tour—458-6149 X515
- White Egret Goat Farm Tour—276-7505 or 276-7408
- Austin Zoo—288-1490
- Great Harvest Bread Tour—329-9216
- The Sanctuary (bird aviary) Tour—288-2199
- Main Post Office Tours (12 & up)—342-1215 or contact your branch
- Central Market Kids Days—206-1000 (every Monday 2-4pm)
- Wild Basin Preserve—327-7622 (call for diverse list of events)
- Bicycle Safety Presentation—708-0513 (for group presentation)
- Volunteer at KLRU, the PBS TV station for a fund drive—471-4811
- Develop a scavenger hunt; come up with a list of things to find.
- Adopt a grandparent at a nursing home.
- Adopt a Highway—832-7066
- Take a ride on a glass elevator—Hyatt Hotel, Embassy Suites, Lakeline Mall, Barton Creek Mall.

To order additional copies of **BATS TO BLUEBONNETS**, please send check or money order for $15 per copy ($12.95 plus Texas sales tax and shipping and handling) to:

ALLIE PRESS
2805 Robinson Avenue
Austin, Texas 78722

For VISA or MasterCard orders, please call (512) 990-2448.

About the Authors

South Texas native *Julie Wade* is happily transplanted in Austin, where she is always looking for something new to do with her husband and tiny son.

When not busy appearing in music videos, multiple internet personality, *Ana-Alicia Konstam* , is organizing fun for her husband and friends.

ACTIVITY INDEX

DESTINATION INDEX